Badger
Slang

Also By Niall Edworthy

Otto Eckhart's Ordeal

England: The Official FA History
Lord's: The Home of Cricket
The Second Most Important Job in the Country
Jonah Lomu: A Giant Amongst Men

Main Battle Tank
Planet Darts

The Optimist/Pessimist's Handbook

Badger's Cricket Compendium
Badger's Golf Compendium

The Curious Gardener's Almanac
The Curious Bird Lover's Almanac
The Curious World of Christmas

Football Stories: Bad Boys & Hard Men

Badger's Football Slang & Banter

An Illustrated A to Z of Classic and Curious Football Speak

Niall Edworthy

Illustrations by Mudd Bexley

Publisher: Badger Books

Copyright: © Niall Edworthy

Niall Edworthy has asserted his right under the Copyright, Designs
and Patents Act 1988 to be identified as the author of this work

All illustrations copyright: © Mudd Bexley

ISBN: 978-1-7384522-62

eBook ISBN:978-1-7384522-79

Book design by Principal Publishing

nialledworthy.com

Ref – Often short, busy little man with a whistle in his mouth, two watches, a notebook and a deck of cards who gives up his weekend afternoons and weekday evenings in order to be abused by thousands of strangers

Get In the Face – Ugly expression for the combative attitude of a team, conjuring images of a drunk man standing on your toes in a pub holding a pool cue or empty pint glass

Honeymoon Period – The period of two or three weeks after a club ties the knot with an attractive new manager before the disappointment sets in and the rowing kicks off. See Also **New Manager Bounce**

Hammer Thrower, Real – Almost obsolete term for a massive bloke at the back, good for nothing but crunching dainty forwards and smashing the ball into **Row Zed**. See **Big Old Unit, Colossus, Physical Freak, Powerhouse**

CONTENTS

Foreword

THIS BOOK IS A bit of harmless fun to be left lying around the house and dipped into for a quick laugh, but it is also the register of a very distinct dialect, the idioms and vernacular of Britain's rich and ancient football culture. I can't believe I have just written that -- about a book that gives definitions to 'Banger, Absolute' … 'Brown Trouser Time' … 'Dink, Little' … and 'Bouncebackability'.

But it's true!

The language of football, clichés and all, is a living tongue - if you'll excuse that – a universal dialect spoken by fans of all strips and stripes. The followers of the game, no matter how much they might detest each other on match day, like it or not, are all bound and united as a 'community' by the words and phrases being used at both ends of the ground, up in the commentary box, in the tunnel and down in the dressing room after the match.

Language gives the tribe its voice by which all its members identify. The tribe may have many clans, but they all speak the same lingo. No one else but a British football fan will ever be heard to say, 'Bang to rights, that was a nailed-on pen. How's the muppet not seen that?'

If you find yourself in a meeting with someone for the first time, struggling to find a connection, and then establish that the other person is a football fan, you've found your common ground and means of communication. That'll be happening right now, up and down the country, two strangers lapsing into 'football speak', forming a little bond and then going on their way.

Right, that's quite enough claims to serious and important cultural study. This is a very silly book. I hope you enjoy dipping into it as much as I enjoyed compiling it.

NE, August 2024

A

Absorbing – Of a game yet to produce a goal and the commentator is eager no one switches over at the break

Acres – Space the size of a prairie in which the lone striker finds himself with only the keeper to beat

Add Some Steel - What the **Enforcer** brings to an otherwise wet midfield that's good only for the fancy creative stuff. See Also **Puts Himself About, Guvnor, Hardman**

Added Time – The unofficial third period of the game getting longer by the year to make up for time lost to amateur dramatics. See Also **Stoppage Time, Injury Time**

Adjudge – Occasionally 'deemed' but never 'considered', if a player is going to stray offside, he prefers his error to be adjudged

Adrift at the Foot – Cliché of mixed metaphors conjuring images both of a boat that has lost its moorings and a man lying at the bottom of a cliff

Agricultural – Ugly, no-nonsense hoick of the ball, usually by a defender towards the gantry to clear danger without taking the risk of a neat pass to feet

Air Shot – As in Golf, but even more humiliating -- a wild swing of the boot that fails to make contact with an object 25 per cent larger than the average human head

All at Sea – When a team has lost its bearings, has no idea where it's heading and is in danger of sinking

All Hands to the Pump – Another nautical expression describing a team adrift or **All at Sea** desperately trying not to **Ship** more goals

Almost Hit That Too Well – A phrase that doesn't make the slightest bit of sense, but everyone knows what the commentator means. Usually of a cleanly struck shot that fails to find the curve or dip that would have led to a goal

Ankle Snapper – A terrible career-threatening tackle. See Also **Studs-Up Tackle, Leave the Foot In**

Aplomb – Since the mid-20th century a word uttered only by football commentators, describing a goal scorer netting with swagger and composure under pressure. Other end of style spectrum from **They All Count**

Argy Bargy – Playground pushing, shoving and shirt-grabbing, usually at a corner or in the defensive wall

Arrive – As a noun, as in a well-timed one, 'a nice arrive' at the back **Stick**

Asking Questions – The main question being: can you carry on playing like that so we can have a goal soon, please?

Assistant Referee – Ambitious, thick-skinned officious type running up and down the line, flapping a flag, a man with dreams of becoming the **Man in the Middle**

happy to spend an afternoon being called a 'F***ing useless, blind w***er!'

Attacking Mid – Fancy, all-skills player **In the Hole**, probably the club's most valuable asset

Authority, Stamping – When a dominant team registers its power over the helpless figures before it like a customs official hammering a stamp into an inkpad

'Ave It! – Bellowed exhortation by a teammate or fans, instructing a player to deposit the ball into Row Zed and clear the danger, or have a shot on goal

AWOL – When a player hasn't **Turned Up on the Day**, his presence almost unnoticeable

Axe, Facing the – The sound of knives being sharpened is just the warning; the axe is the club's weapon of choice for dispatching the manager. See Also **Heads Will Roll**

B

Back of the Net! – The gleeful cry of commentator and fan

Backbone – The virtue all teams need to stiffen resolve and provide structure. Without one, your performance will be **Spineless** and lacking that little bit of **Character**

Backs-to-the-Wall Stuff – When a team is **Under the Cosh** and showing some **Backbone**. See **Rearguard Action**

Bad Day at the Office – Shrugging off the setback of defeat like it's no big deal, we all have them

Bag of Nails – When the set-up of a team is a mess, or the structure has gone to pot. Players all over the place, out of position

Ball to Feet – Where every pass should go in an ideal world

Ball Boy– Lucky young lad – or lass - who gets a free ticket and the best seat in the house for chucking the ball back

Ball-Watching – When a dozy defender is daydreaming, watching the build-up of play, and not the man who has ghosted in behind him to score

Bang to Rights – When the law offers no mitigation to the offending player who has hacked the legs off an opponent or grabbed at the ball like it was netball

B a n g e r / B e a u t y, Absolute – See Also **Scorcher, Belter, Thunderbolt, Screamer**

Banging Them In – Describing a team or player on a hot goal-scoring streak, a whole level above 'knocking them in.' **See Also Scoring Goals for Fun**

Banter, Bit of – Making light of the vile abuse being exchanged between players

Bar – i) Crossbar ii) Where the players head as soon as they've showered

Basement, Down in the – Where lowly clubs facing eviction to a lower division live

Beach Football – A compliment if the team are winning at their leisure, but derogatory if they're losing and playing like they're mucking around on holiday

Beach, On the – Where players spend their summers talking to their agents from a lounger

Beaver – Industrious midfielder. Usually short with a shiny coat, brilliant at building dams

Bed, Put to – The goal that all but seals victory and fans can sleep tight

Beleaguered – Britain's 'Beleaguered' Community is made up mainly of football clubs and football managers

Belter – A brilliant goal or game. See Also **Banger/ Beauty, Scorcher, Screamer**

Bench Warmer – Substitute. Phrase soon to be upgraded to Ergonomic Padded Armchair Warmer

Benched – Not to be confused with **Subbed**, this refers to a player starting the game as a substitute, often because he has upset the manager

Best Interests of the Club – Diplomatic gloss on the sacking of a hopeless manager

Bicycle Kick – Spectacular circus trick right out of the **Top Drawer** when a player turns himself upside down in midair with his back to goal and hard pedals the ball into the net. 'Overhead kick' just doesn't quite capture the drama of the act

Big, Make Himself – Miraculous inflation of a goalkeeper before a penalty kick

Big Ask – The massive challenge of a **Minnow** squaring up against a giant

Big Game Player – One who can't be bothered against the lesser teams, but when there's a full house, the game is on telly and the opposition is worth some effort, he will drag himself off the couch, step onto the stage and put on a performance

Big Old Unit – Physically imposing often unskilled player at the back or **Up Top**. See Also **Colossus, Rock, Old-Fashioned Nine**

Bigger than the Club, No One – Reference to a massive narcissist in the ranks undermining the collective

Bit of Quality, That Little – What a player has if he can do a step-over

Blaze – Meteoric shot over the crossbar leaving a trail of luminous debris

Blinder – An absolutely brilliant performance usually by an individual not a team. Origin of phrase probably, 'God Blind Me!'

Blistering Pace – When a player is so fast, the heat generated is so intense that the skin of the man trying to mark him will break out in watery pustules. See Also **Flying Machine, Genuine Pace, Jet-heeled, Speed Merchant**

Blow - A chance … a lead … a game wide open … blow away … job in the car park

Blushes, Sparing– Late goal for the supposedly superior team

Bogey Team – Shit team that always beats a better one. See Also **Hoodoo**

Booking – When the ref has the job satisfaction of taking out his policeman's notepad and writing out a ticket for a misdemeanour

Boot Boy – Do they still exist? Young player learning his place in the pecking order by cleaning the muck off the senior players' footwear

Boots (Filling them) – Like the soldiers from a bygone era grabbing as much loot as possible, a team will see rich pickings and grab, er, a hatful of easy goals

Bore Draw – Very dull game that wasted everyone's afternoon and money

Born out of Frustration – When a player commits a hideous challenge because he's fed up with having the mickey taken out of him by a superior performer

Bottle It – When a player or team throws away an opportunity through a loss of nerve or guts

Bouncebackability – Ugly German-style compound word for a team or player's capacity to deal with setbacks

Box – i) Penalty area ii) Penning a team or player in a small area of the pitch

Boxing Day – Traditional round of fixtures on the day after Christmas when the male of the species cannot get down to his pre-match pub fast enough

Box-to-box – All-action midfielder, slide-tackling in his own box to save the day one minute, sweeping home an **Absolute Banger** at the other end moments later

Bragging Rights – When the bitter local rivals are beaten, and you can sing about it all night down the pub

Brand of Football – Grand way of saying a team either plays a passing game or takes the **Long Ball** approach

Bread-and-Butter – Of a goalkeeper's simple save to deny a striker a **Meat-and-Drink** opportunity

Break Forward – Do teams ever break towards their own goal?

(The) Break – Half-time interval when, in the old days, players had 15 minutes to enjoy a fag and a quarter of an orange. Today, it's an opportunity to **Take on Fluids** and enjoy a good **Rub Down**

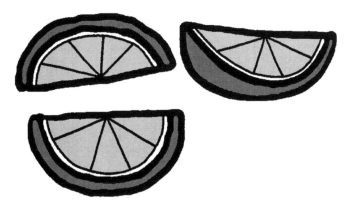

Brown Trouser Time – Penalty shootout

Buffet Ball – A great pass and the striker helps himself

Building from the Back – Slightly meaningless expression. Hard to build moves from the front

Bullet – Usually of a powerful header, sometimes of a pass and occasionally of a shot

Bundle – a) Scramble the ball over the line b) All-in wrangle amongst the players, pulling shirts and calling each other names

Bung – Unauthorised payment to an agent or manager or the player himself to secure a transfer. A popular pastime in 1970s motorway service stations

Buried – Of a well-taken shot or a well-beaten team

Bursting Blood Vessels – ... to get on the end of a ball with an extraordinary aerobic effort that risks the eruption of arteries and veins

Buy a Goal, Inability to – When a team is playing so poorly and created not the breath of a chance on goal

Buy a Ticket (Need to) – If a player or team wants to enter the raffle and win the prize of a goal, they must buy tickets by taking shots, as in ice hockey ace Wayne Gretsky's famous quote: 'You miss 100% of the shots you don't take.'

C

Cagey – Commentator euphemism for a desperately dull start to a game when the ball gets passed sideways and backwards for so long everyone wishes they never left the pub

Cakewalk – When the result is no longer in doubt and the winners are **Scoring Goals for Fun**. Refers to old custom in Deep South when dancers won cake for the best strutting

Camped in the Opposition Half – When a team has dug in with everything but tents and billycans, laying siege to the goal

Caning, A Good – What an authoritarian team dishes out to a helpless little one

Cap – i) Appearance for the national team for which the player receives a small hat they would never dare wear in public ii) Late goal to seal a great day out

Captain Marvel – Skipper with superpowers who can ghost through defensive walls, move mountains, blister skin with his pace and produce a **Moment of Magic** of which mere mortals can only dream

Card-happy Ref – Like the grinning traffic warden, a type of sinister match official who just loves catching transgressors, throwing the book at them and ruining the game for everyone. It's why he does it

Caressed – Quasi-erotic description for a pass that has been lovingly stroked to a favourite teammate

Caretaker – i) Interim manager who will be in post for about a week ii) Guy who cleans the club bogs and has done for 40 years but no one knows his name

Carpet – Playing surface, usually a beautifully manicured one with a pattern of squares and none of that beastly 1970s mud. What the fancy teams like to pass it about on

Catalogue – Football has two catalogues, one for injuries, one for errors

Catenaccio – Tedious Italian word people use to sound cultured for a tactical system that means little more than playing with a tight defence. It's not so fancy in Italy where it means, simply, 'door-bolt'

Caught Napping – Of a dozy player or defence who has drifted out of the **Wide-Awake Club**

Cauldron – A small, packed stadium boiling over with passionate partisan support

Channels, In the – Notional tramlines running between fullbacks and central defenders into which strikers are encouraged to run and midfielders to pass. See Also **Gullies**

Chances Go Begging – God bless you, guv, please just stick me in the back of the net

Chant – Ritual football songs of the terrace, often irreverent and mocking, never to be confused with Gregorian chant

Character – Never specific about the type of character his team has displayed, this is what a manager claims the lads had shown for the full 90 minutes

Chase Shadows – The purgatorial fate of an overwhelmed midfield

Cheaply – Giving the ball away at bargain basement prices

Cheeky – An impudent goal or piece of skill

Chip – Technical term for **Little Dink**

Chop – Hideous, scything tackle popular in the 1970s

Christmas Tree – The 4–5–1 team formation that bears a dim resemblance to the Festive evergreen owing to the pointy bit or star up top

Clanger – Awful mistake that has led to a goal. See Also **Howler**

Class Act – Of any player with above-average skills

Clatter – Onomatopoeic word to describe a tough challenge

Clean Sheet – When the goalkeeper and defence have gone about their housekeeping and left a tidy scoresheet

Clearance – A hoof up field or into the stands, or a mad scramble near the goal line

Clear-out, Good – When the club sweeps its useless, underperforming overpaid players into the street or onto the transfer market, often after the arrival of a new broom in the manager's office

Clinical– Of a finish, act of skill or team performance that would bring pride to an operating theatre by its precision and efficiency

Clueless – Usually of a defender with his mouth hanging open staring at the ball nestled in the netting

Clumsy More Than Anything – Of a reckless challenge by a bovine defender

Coasting – When a side is 3-0 up with half an hour to go, and the game is over as a contest and spectacle

Coat of Paint – Long having replaced 'cigarette paper', this remains the preferred unit of measurement to define a very close shave with an upright

Collector's Item – When the 38-year-old centre-back and club stalwart hits home with a wild swing of the boot from outside the box

Colossus – … at the back. See Also **Rock, Big Old Unit, Physical Freak, Hammer Thrower, Powerhouse**

Comedy of Errors – Go-to commentator's description of any defensive mix-up. See Also **Shambolic at the Back**

Coming-Together – Less than a full collision, more than a mere brush or tangle

Compact – When a team is using only about a third of the pitch and believe that loads of quick little five-yard passes will make them look like a thinking man's continental outfit

Composed in Front of Goal – Doesn't have a panic attack and blaze over

Comprehensive – Not quite a thrashing, usually a win by three goals

Consolation Goal – When a losing team scores a goal that has no impact on the final result, and they are said to be comforted by that

Contenders, Real – Uttered with a hint of surprise because the team described never win anything and no one will quite believe it if they finally do

Conveyor Belt – Generation of talented youngsters coming through the academy of a club like cans of high-quality baked beans off a production line

Conviction – Always of the need to show more on the pitch

Corridor of Uncertainty – Vivid term borrowed from cricket to describe a cross or pass into the awkward area between the goalkeeper and his defenders that wins half a second of time for the striker to pounce

Corker – Pleasing, old-fashioned comic strip word for a great goal

Cotton Wool, Player Wrapped In – If the team's best player is carrying a bit of a knock ahead of a crucial match, his manager will wrap him in soft, fluffy material and put him in a little box to make sure no further harm comes to him

Counter-pressing – A bit of an overblown, nonsense term to describe the usual ebb and flow of a game

Coup – In football, only a transfer can be a coup unless someone is head-butted by a French player in which case there has been a Coup de Tête

Crash Out – In for a penny, in for a pound … if you are going to be eliminated from a cup competition then to hell with it, you might as well crash out

Creeping into our Game, This sort of Thing – No one wants to see it. A commonly heard expression in the 1990s revealing a xenophobic fear of dark practices found on the Continent and South America e.g. Playacting, professional fouls, begging the ref to send a player off, making diving gestures. The English have always preferred their wrongdoing to be plain as a pikestaff and therefore fair

Cricket Score – A massive exaggeration when a team goes two-up early in the game, 'This could be a...' What, like 467 for 8 declared?

Crisp – Passes are either crisp or sloppy

Cross (Awkward one to Deal With) – When the goalkeeper has to make a bit of an effort and jump in the air to gather

Crowd Pleaser – A player who will go largely unnoticed for most of the match and then do a **Seal Dribble** and find himself the toast of the town

Crowd Scene – Packed goalmouth

Crown Jewels – When a player has been whacked in the gonads and the commentator wants to keep it polite

Cruising – When a team has reached the heights, is out of sight and flicked on the autopilot

Crunch Game – A telling encounter between two rivals, either vying for a title or a promotion spot or to avoid relegation

Crunching Tackle – When a player concertinas his opponent with a heavy challenge

Cultured Left Foot – A foot that studied Moral Philosophy and Fine Art at Uni

C**t Punt – Terrible swipe at the ball skewing high and wide into the stands

Cupset – Neat little addition to football's lexicon, sure to become a well-worn cliché, when an act of **Giant-killing** has taken place

Curly Finger – What the manager gives a player about to be substituted, or the ref a player about to be carded

Custodian – Slightly naff, pompous term for a goalkeeper

Cynical – A sneaky foul somehow considered more shameful than a brutal and blatant one. See Also **Professional Foul**

D

Daisy Cutter – Fast low shot that mows the heads off small flowers

Danger Zone – Statement of the obvious referring to the area where most goals are scored

Dangerous Lead – An oxymoron, but veteran football fans will get the half-truth of it. The most dangerous lead is probably the one taken very early in the game

Dark Horses – Solid cliché, borrowed from horse racing, dating back to the nineteenth century. The unlikely team no one believed would be at the races when the competition began

David and Goliath – When a backwater club plays one of the giants from the big city, and all neutrals get behind the provincial part-timers who all drive milk floats and work as postmen during the week

Dead & Buried - … only to come back to life as if by a miracle

Dead Man Walking – Only a manager can be a dead man walking and he will probably be killed with 'the axe'

Deep – 1) When a team takes up a line of defence closer towards their goal, usually

to reduce space for a team with fast, attacking players
ii) Of Gareth Southgate and other thoughtful managers
with pained faces

Defensive Mid – Midfielder in front of line of defence,
there to **Mind the House**, while others go off on their
travels and have some fun. See Also **Libero, Sweeper**

Deft – Of a touch

Denied by the Post – When the upright refuses entry
to the goal

Dent – Usually in title hopes

Derby – Match between two, usually local, rivals. Origins
uncertain, possibly after the 12th Earl of Derby

Derisory – Only an offer for a player can be derisory
in football. Salaries are never derisory, nor the costs of
building a new stadium

Desmond – Rhyming slang for a 2-2 draw, after
Archbishop Desmond Tutu, South African bishop and
anti-apartheid campaigner

Dethrone – Defending champions can be removed
from a throne just like monarchs

Dig, Have a – Encouraging a player to take a shot

Dig In – When the battle intensifies, and the defending team gets out the entrenching tools to deal with waves of attack

Dink, Little – An impudent little **Chip** often over a sprawling goalkeeper

Dirty Work – Work undertaken in the midfield by the unglamorous, stocky fella. See Also **Beaver, Packhorse, Workhorse, Grafter**

Disaster, Recipe for – When all the ingredients in the mix point to an unsavoury outcome e.g. when a make-shift team features players in unfamiliar positions

Disciplinary Tightrope, Walking a - The commentator's imagination pictures a player wobbling on a high wire at risk of a painful fall when he is one bad challenge away from a red card or missing the next game in a major tournament

Dispatch – Like a mafia hit job, a team will neutralise the opposition with a minimum of fuss or conscience, finishing the job with a **Killer** goal

Dive, Take a – One of football's deadly sins: deceiving the ref by falling to the ground sneakily or collapsing with a theatrical flourish in order to win a free kick or penalty

Do a Job – A good solid day at the office. When players or a team clock in, whistle while they work, do what they get paid for without complaint or mishap, clock out and go home to the Missus, job done, laters. See Also **Workmanlike**

Do a Leeds – When a club is brought low by its over-ambition, splashing the cash like its Monopoly money under the self-entitled illusion they are still a big player because they had a good ten years a generation or so earlier. Leeds United reached the Champions League semi-finals in 2001; six years later they were playing Yeovil in League One

Donkey – Ungainly ass of a player, usually at the back

Don't Fancy it – Of a team not showing as much desire as the other

Down Like He was Shot, Goes – When a player, barely brushed by an opponent, drops like a **Sack of Spuds** in the pathetic hope of winning a penalty or free kick

Draw Written All Over It – The inevitable deadlock when two teams are **Cagey** from start to finish

Dressing Room, He's Lost the – When the players realise the manager's a dick, conjuring images of silence and sullen faces on the benches around the lockers

Dribbling – Old-fashioned craft of beating a sequence of players with close control. Lighter balls, fitter players and the realisation that a ball will cover more ground if it is passed have led to a decline in this ancient art. Once a Roy of the Rovers hero, today a dribbler is more likely to be considered a ball-hog or show-off

Drilled – A ball that has been struck with tremendous force

Drop Zone - Relegation area

Droves – Droves can never enter a ground, only leave it early

Drubbing, Proper – A half-hearted drubbing is just not the same

Dugout – Little bus stop of a hut with a plastic roof where unwanted players warm benches

Dummy – Beginner's conjuring trick by which a player fools his gullible opponent, feinting one way but going the other

Dumped Unceremoniously - If a club is to be dumped from the Cup, it must be done without elaborate ritual

Dying Breed – Of a player from the Palaeolithic era, probably smokes and drinks hard

Dynamo – Of a scrapping midfielder who hares around after more talented opponents. See Also **Scrapper, Puts Himself About, Grafter, Beaver**

E

Eagle-eyed – Only a **Referee's Assistant** can be eagle-eyed

Early Bath – Where the fuming player banished from the **Field of Play** is said to be heading, his mood not improved when he discovers that the team communal bath was replaced by showers about half a century ago

Early Doors – The opening period of a match. From days when pubs shut in the afternoon and drinkers came back for the evening sesh

Easy Street – Where a dominant team lives

Egg – Cartoon swelling from a knock usually to the thigh

El Clásico – Derby match between leading teams in Spanish-speaking countries

Elevator Team – A club always in a promotion or relegation scrap, bouncing between two divisions with regularity. See Also **Yo-Yo** club

Eleventh Hour – You cannot score a goal at the eleventh hour, but you can be transferred to another club at that time

Embarrassment of Riches – Red-faced clubs hogging all the best players

Encroach – When players sneak into the penalty box ready for the rebound at a penalty kick

End-to-End Stuff – All-action game loved by neutrals, nerve-jangling for the partisans

End Product – Naff way of saying 'Goal'

Enforcer – See **Guvnor, Add Steel, Scrapper, Hardman**

Engine Room – The components of the midfield doing all the work and making the team tick

Enter the Fray – A substitute joins the combat to bolster his embattled comrades

European Night – Obsolete expression from the days when a midweek match against continental opposition was a rare treat

Every Blade of Grass – Every last one covered by the team's manic little midfield dynamo

Every Game is a Cup Final Now – When a result is needed from every remaining match to avoid relegation or clinch the title

Exocet - A shot that travels like the French-built anti-ship missile, the phrase entering football commentary usage after the 1982 Falklands War. See Also **Howitzer**

Eye for Goal – Keen-sighted player who can unerringly pick out the 24 x 8-foot structure with a net hanging off the back

Eyes in the Back of His Head – Victorian Freak Show of a player who knows exactly what's going on to his rear

F

Fall from Grace – Not from God's Grace but, more importantly, from the manager's good offices, and the player soon finds himself **Surplus to Requirements**

Fall Kindly – When the ball has the good manners to land perfectly for a decent shot on goal

False Nine – A centre forward who drops back into midfield to foil his man-marker and create space for other attackers

Family Club – Where there's less fighting and throwing of objects

Fan Park – Area away from the match venue – often in city centres – for drinking, fighting and watching a big game on a massive television screen

Fans' Favourite – Consistent, long-serving player or a new and exciting kid on the block

Farmers' League – Derogatory term for non-league football or of a side playing poorly. See Also **Pub Team, Sunday League**

Feeder Club – A smaller club that gives all its best players to a bigger one

Fergie Time – Excessive injury time, especially for a home side, from the popular perception that refs, worried by the prospect of the **Hair Dryer Treatment** from manager Sir Alex 'Taggart' Ferguson, would stick on a few extra minutes to give Manchester United a bit longer to level or win

Felt That, He – Commentator understatement when a player has been pulverised in the challenge

Field of Play – Quaintly old-fashioned expression for the pitch

Fifty-fifty – A challenge for the ball that will often leave one player rolling around the floor clutching his lower leg

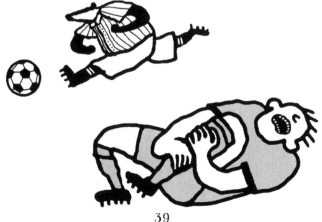

Final Throw of the Dice – When the goalkeeper lumbers up field like a giraffe and joins the ten outfield players in a desperate last bid for a goal

Final Whistle – Old-school for full-time

Finish – Score a goal, usually ending a decent move

Fire, On – When a player is on such a hot streak, he might as well be engulfed in flames

Fire Home – Sharp finish, as opposed to sweep or poke home

First Rule of Defending – If in doubt, hoof it into the stands

First Touch – … is the sweetest. A 'good first touch' is the pre-requisite skill of the top player

Fish Up a Tree – Player who doesn't fit in at a club

Fixture Congestion – Like traffic, the backlog of games that builds up, provoking anxiety and curses

Flag – i) What the **Line-o** waves around ii) The pennant in the four angles of the pitch iii) What dispirited teams do in the second half against Man City

Flair Player – The one with the most skill who will score a **Blinder** from time to time

Flapped at It – What a keeper is said to do in mid-air when he can't quite reach the ball or is being obstructed from doing so

Flat-footed – Describing a slow, shit player being given the runaround by a far superior one, usually of a defender or an entire defence

Flat Back Four – Defenders formed up in a ramrod straight line across the pitch, nothing fancy like you find on the Continent

Flattered Them a Little, The Scoreline - When a team has been battered and the losing manager thinks 3-0 would have been fairer than 5-0

Flea in the Ear – What an under-performing or troublesome player can expect to feel when being ticked off by the **Gaffer**

Flick-on, Little – When a player helps the ball on to a colleague with the merest touch

Flier, Off to a – Goals **Early Doors**, game over before it gets going

Floodgates – These are thrown open to release a torrent of goals

Fluffed His Lines – Like an actor at the National, what a player is said to do when he misses an easy chance, and can expect no sympathy from the cheap seats

Flurry – Multiple yellow cards dispensed in a short period of time come in flurries, falling from a sky like, er, yellow snow

Flying Machine – Fast winger. See Also **Blistering Pace, Genuine Pace, Jet-Heeled, Speed Merchant**

Foot off the Gas – When a team or player gets complacent or lazy or doesn't **Fancy It**

(The) Footie – The vernacular for football. Are you going to or watching …?'

Footrace – In contrast to the other one performed on the hands at speed

Forlorn Figure, Cuts a – The striker who has missed a hatful of chances, the defender who has fired into his own net or the keeper who has let one through his legs

Form Out the Window – Good form never takes the door. It likes to clamber through a window

Fortress – Ground with crenelated battlements and arrow slits inhabited by a team boasting a strong home form

Fortuitous – Happening by chance, wrong word for 'fortunate'

Four-Four-Two – Classic, old-school team formation adopted by British teams for the better part of a century before continental influences began **Creeping Into Our Game.** See Also **Flat Back Four**

Fourth Official – The guy being shouted at by managers in and around the technical area

Fox in the Box – An expression only in usage because it rhymes. Foxes don't play football. See Also **Goal Poacher**

Freak Injury – Usually occurring away from the pitch, e.g. when a player drops a bottle of ketchup on his foot or steps on a skateboard in the dark

Fresh Legs – The introduction of substitutions to replace tired ones, straight from the fridge of the bench

Friendly – Is there such a thing? Better perhaps to call it a non-competitive match or a warm-up game

Fringe Player – One who only gets a game in an injury pandemic and will be transferred to a lower league club the moment anyone shows any interest

Full Gun – Powerful shot

Fun, Scoring Goals for – When an in-form striker skips around laughing his head off, just **Banging Them In**

Funny Old Game – Catch-all expression, perhaps the greatest of all football clichés, uttered after any unusual development in the game or fate of a team

G

Gaffer – The Manager. Word believed to a phonetic reduction of Godfather from back in the day

Galactico – Originally to describe any huge new signing by Real Madrid, then any top Spanish player and now any world-class player

Galaxy of Stars – Inevitable metaphor to describe a team with a great many good players

Game of Two Halves - In which the fortunes of a team have reversed at the interval. Real contender, with **Funny Old Game** or **Sick as a Parrot,** for greatest ever football cliché. Like many clichés, it perfectly describes the events that have unfolded. It's just been used so much it's lost the power of its meaning

Gantry – Where frozen TV commentators sit, and centre-backs clear the ball

Gave it 110 per cent, The Lads – If a team or player has pushed themselves to the limit of their endurance, they have either given it 100% or 110%. No other numeral can convey the effort expended

Gears – Going through them, always from low to high. Teams are never said to go down through the gears and park in neutral

Genuine Pace – As opposed to the fake stuff you can buy online from China. See Also **Blistering Pace, Jet-heeled, Flying Machine, Speed Merchant**

Get In the Face – Ugly expression for combative attitude of a team, conjuring images of a drunk man standing on your toes in a pub holding a pool cue or empty pint glass

Get Stuck In – One notch down in intensity from **Get In the Face**

Ghost – When a player passes through a defence or around another player, an ethereal phantom from another dimension sending shudders down the spines of the fans

Ghost Goal – When the ball crosses the goal line but is not given or is given when it hasn't. See Also **Phantom Goal**

Giant of the Game – Massive player, at least seven foot tall, who towers over the common workman dwarves of the game. Often Immortal. Can also walk on water and through walls. Gets free pints everywhere. See Also **Legend**

Giant-killing – When David downs Goliath with club resources the equivalent of a poxy slingshot

Gilt-edged – An opportunity to score so good it comes plated with precious metal

Give-and-Go, Little – Lay the ball off to a mate, run three yards, get the ball back. Your Dad called it a **One-Two**

Go Shopping – When the **Attacking Mid** teams up with the forwards to hunt a goal while the Defensive Mid **Minds the House** at the back

Goal-hanger – A sight rarely seen in organised football since the introduction of the offside rule in 1863, but a common one in a game of Jumpers-for-Goals, the lazy figure standing around with his hands in his pockets waiting for a ball to tap in

Goalkeepers' Union – Like the Fast Bowlers' Union in cricket, this is a mythical institution to which no one has ever belonged. Have you ever seen men in lurid green or pink tops warming their hands over a barrel stove?

Goal Poacher – The poacher works with speed and guile to outfox the gamekeepers. See Also **Fox in the Box**

Goalmouth Scramble – When the action in the six-yard box goes kinetic and comic, the ball pinging around like it's in a tombola, players leap and flail, throw themselves to the ground and kick out in all directions, commentators screech and wet themselves and the fans of the defending side yell, 'F***ing hoof it!'

Golazo – Another Continental expression **Creeping into the Game**, this one to describe a spectacular goal

Golden Generation – Golden Shower more like, in England's case. No Golden Generation has ever brought home a trophy

Good Feet – Nonsense expression to describe a player showing a few basic skills for which he is paid handsomely, like trapping the ball with his first touch

Got Away with That – Of a team's result, or an error that didn't lead to disaster. See Also **Great Escape**

Grafter – The name given to the most unskilful player in the side who makes up for a lack of natural talent with a lot of hard work. See Also **Workhorse, Piano Carrier, Dirty Work, Beaver, Packhorse**

Greasy Surface – The quality of a football pitch after a bit of rain. N.B. Always greasy, never slippery

Great Advert for the Game – Like football needs any more fans. Give the other sports a chance! Cristiano Ronaldo alone has almost 850 million social media followers

Great Bit of Business – When a club has got the better of the transfer negotiations and bought a good player for a bargain or sold an average one for **Silly Money**

Great Escape – When a plucky team tunnels its way out of trouble for an unlikely draw or win. An escape must always be Great. See Also **Got Away with That**

Grind Out a Result – To play terribly but get a point

Groin, Feeling A – When a player is carrying a slight limp

Groundhoppers – Football equivalent of train spotters. Badge-Boy hobby of travelling the country and beyond 'collecting' visits to football grounds. A.k.a. Hoppers.

Grudge Game – A match to avenge some previous injustice in the fixture or a traditional hate-fest between two clubs with 'history' e.g. QPR v Luton, Palace v Brighton or any game with Millwall

Gullies – The area of the pitch roughly between full-backs and centre-backs where forwards want the Mids to knock balls. See Also **Channels**

Gutted – Emotional condition of a team or a player after an ill-deserved defeat or failure to achieve a prize

Guvnor – Hard-nut midfielder, usually the Defensive Mid, who only plays the game to bully people. See **Add Some Steel, Puts Himself About, Hardman, Enforcer**

H

Hailing a Taxi – What a keeper is said to be doing when he rushes off the line flapping in vain to collect a cross

Hair Dryer Treatment – What a manager does to his players in the dressing room at half-time or after an abject display, leaning into faces and blasting them with hot invective. Ex-Man United boss Alex Ferguson is said to have had the turbo model, but managers have been spraying the spittle since the days of steel toecaps

Half a Yard – Commentator's measurement to describe any short distance

Hallowed Turf – Medieval church expression meaning 'holy' to describe the playing surface at Wembley. No other football pitch has sacred sod

Hammer – i) To beat a team by a very big margin ii) A player or follower of West Ham United

Hammer Blow – When a side concedes a late goal after an otherwise encouraging day, they experience exactly the same sensation as when they flatten their thumb with a hammer. Fact

Hammer Thrower, Real – Almost obsolete term for a massive bloke at the back, good for nothing but crunching dainty forwards and smashing the ball into **Row Zed**. See **Big Old Unit, Colossus, Physical Freak, Powerhouse**

Hammie, Pulled a – When the hamstring goes, the player reaches for a buttock and hops around grimacing

Hand of God – An expression that just won't go away. Describing Diego Maradona's first goal against England in the 1986 World Cup when he palmed the ball into the net, 40 years on, it is trotted out at every reference to Argentina and the player himself

Handbags – Playground pushing and shoving, pulling shirts and going toe-to-toe. Distinct from 'handbags' in rugby where the term is used euphemistically to describe a mass brawl with blood

Handful, Proving to be a – Of a player making a nuisance of himself up front, or a supposedly inferior team putting up a good fight

Hang Up One's Boots – Managers 'call it a day' but players put their footwear on a peg in the dressing room before going to open a pub

Hang Your Hat On – What you can do with the big, towering centre-forward suspended in mid-air waiting for a ball to head home

Hard Man – Less common today in an age of fancier football, but every British club used to have a player prized not for his skills but his ability to intimidate, clatter and maim opponents. See Also **Guvnor, Add Some Steel, Enforcer**

Hardy Souls – The four away supporters at Blackpool on a Tuesday night in November

Head!, On the – Striker's command to his winger

Headache To Have, Nice – When the star player returns from injury, but the team is playing really well without him

Headless Chicken – Hapless midfielder out of his depth running around in circles

Heads will Roll – Similar to the situation in which the nobility of Revolutionary France found themselves. Clueless managers, pointless coaches and underperforming, overpaid players will pay for their cruel indifference to the fans with a trip to the guillotine

Heavy Metal – Phrase introduced to the lexicon by Liverpool manager Jurgen Klopp to describe a brand of football that is fast, intense and overpowering. See Also **High Octane**

High Foot – When a player goes in studs-up above the knee and will likely be shown a card coloured red

High Octane – When a team is pumping on all cylinders fuelled by their own excellence. See Also **Heavy Metal**

High, Wide and Not Very Handsome – Of a shot that has veered crazily towards the corner flag. See Also **It's not Rugby!**

His Face Says it All – When a manager is enduring a wretched **Day at the Office,** the cameraman shows him on the touchline with a face like a **Wet Wednesday Night in Wigan**

His Head's Not Right – Of a player who has gone **AWOL** wandering around the pitch quoting the Bible to himself

Hit Stride – What teams do when they wake up and start to play some proper football

Holding Role/Holding Midfielder – Central midfielder with the job of protecting the defence and providing a link to the guys with the fancy skills higher up the pitch. The holding midfielder is often tall and strolls around like he owns the place

Hold Our Hands Up - Like good honest schoolboys who have been in mischief, players will own up to their wrongdoing on the pitch

Hold Up the Ball – When a defender is pressing into his backside flailing kicks at his ankles, the **Old Fashioned Nine** shields the ball, waiting for teammates to show up on the scene, or slow down play for the final whistle

Hole – The mystical space on a pitch between the midfielders and the forwards. A team setup in a 3-5-1-1 formation has a 'player in the hole'

Hollywood Ball – A spectacular **Raking Pass** from one end or side of the pitch to the other

Home, Romping – Like a frothing racehorse with its tongue out the side of its mouth, what a side is said to be doing when it's banging in the goals towards the end of the game

Honeymoon Period – The period of two or three weeks after a club ties the knot with an attractive new manager before the disappointment sets in and the rowing kicks off. See Also **New Manager Bounce**

Hoodoo – The curse that one team, often an inferior one, holds over another. See Also **Bogey Team**

Hoof – Agricultural punt up field or into the stands to clear the ball. Occasionally, a game strategy deployed by managers without time for all that elaborate continental stuff

Hoolies – Hooligans. Like Morris Dancers, only more violent. Revivalist 1970s and 1980s movement, its members keeping the past alive by congregating at train stations and pre-arranged car parks and pubs to knock lumps out of their Neanderthal mates from a rival tribe

Horror Tackle – Hideous challenge that might well have maimed its victim and curtailed his career

Hospital Ball/Pass – Under-strength, short ball to a teammate in no space to manoeuvre with a massive **Defensive Mid** bearing down on him at speed

Hot Seat – The manager's seat at the club always comes with built-in heating. The seat is rarely warm, and never stone cold

Howitzer – Erroneous artillery term to describe an explosive shot. Erroneous because the howitzer was designed to fire up and over fortifications, like big mortars. See Also **Exocet**

Howler – Grievous error made by a player or referee usually causing hilarity amongst one half of the fans. See Also **Clanger**

Human, The Ref is – Football fans need to be reminded from time to time that the match official is flesh and blood, prone to failings, just like the rest of us. To prove it, he sometimes has to click the pictures with bicycles or traffic lights in them, then tick a box that says 'I am not a Robot'

Hunting Grounds, Happy – Hunting Grounds are never sad places. After an afternoon galloping about in pursuit of its quarry, the happy hunters always get their kill

Hunting in Packs – When midfielders gang up, harass and menace clueless bystanders

I

Ill-Tempered – It's all kicked off

Implode – A team does what black holes do when all the energy has gone out of their performance

Inept Performance – A manager's cute way of saying they played like shit

Inject – … pace, urgency, tempo, hope, cortisone

Injury time – The ten minutes that it is now customary to add on to **Normal Time** to make up for all the rolling around in agony. See Also **Stoppage Time, Added Time**

Inside Forward – How your grandfather describes an **Attacking Mid**

Insurance Man – Defensive Mid sitting in front of the back four

In Tatters – Of hopes and dreams and defences

In Their Own Hands – Or 'It's Only theirs to Lose.' When a team start as clear favourites in a tie and the commentator lays his jinx

Invisible Man – When a pass is made, and no one is there to receive it

Invite a Foul – 'Please try and break my ankle so I can have a free-kick or a breather on the floor'

Inviting Cross – An incoming ball attractive to a towering centre-forward

It's Not Rugby! – When a player **Blazes** the ball way over the crossbar. See Also **High, Wide and Not So Handsome**

J

Jet-heeled – Of wingers and full-backs who can run faster than the man opposite. See Also **Blistering Pace, Genuine Pace, Flying Machine, Speed Merchant**

Jinking – Of a run with ball at feet when a player goes round at least two players. A player who jinks a lot is a Jinker

Journeyman – Mildly derogatory term for a player who has represented many different clubs over their career i.e. it takes a club a year or two realise he's an average-to-shit footballer and therefore **Surplus to Requirements**. Opposite of **One-Club Man**

Juggling – i) When the keeper plays **Keepie-Uppie** using his fingers ii) When a manager has a team to keep a large squad of entitled prima donnas happy

K

Keepie-Uppie – The art of juggling a football in the air, using all the limbs. A useless skill in a real game, it is often seen performed on beaches and parks and by Dads showing off to their toddlers

Kick and Rush – British style of football for about a century until the show-off continentals started creeping into the game. See Also **Route One**

Kick-Off – i) The start or restart of a match after a goal ii) There's a brawl

Kidology, Little Bit of – Bluffing by the manager, usually over team selection ahead of a big match, in an effort to outfox his opposite man. Usually pointless

Kill the Game – i) The extra goal late on that is certain to seal victory ii) When a team reins in its attacking impulses and runs the clock down for the final whistle

Killer – Usually of a great pass, occasionally of a goal, rarely of a man running around the pitch with a deadly weapon

Kit – The team shorts, shirt and socks worn by players; a new one rolled out at the start of every season in order to fleece fans. See Also **Strip**

Kitchen Sink – What a team fly-tips at a losing cause. The football grounds of Britain are littered with them

Knife and Fork – What an especially good delivery to a striker comes with when a **Meat and Drink** chance has been served him **On a Plate**

Knives Sharpened – The ritual undertaken by reporters and club executives when a failing manager is a game or two from getting the sack. The sharp knives are then put in a drawer and the axe is wielded

Knock – i) Minor injury ii) Minor criticism

Knock it Around – Aimless passing back and forth in the middle of the pitch because the team is on **Easy Street** b) No one is making a decent run or can think of anything creative or clever do

Knockers, He's Got His - A player or manager who does not attract universal favour

Knocking on the Door – … and eventually the defence

will stop pretending they're out and open it. When a team builds pressure and threatens to score. If knocking doesn't work, they start battering on it

Knows Where the Goal Is – Innate gift of the striker able to seek out and identify two uprights, a crossbar with a net hanging off the back

Knuckleball – New expression in football, borrowed from baseball, this is a shot struck with no spin, making it move erratically in the air, hard for the keeper to judge

Kop – A single-tier stand housing home fans, named after the Spion Kop, a steep hillside and scene of the Battle of Spion Kop in the Boer War. Liverpool's is by far the most well-known Kop, but Aston Villa's used to be the largest, holding 30,000 fans. Today, Tottenham Hotspur's is the largest – and steepest – with 17,300.

L

Labour to Victory – When the game has been interminably dull, won by a team who should have done so with greater ease

Laced It – Nice old expression for a powerful shot struck cleanly with the full face of the boot, just as it says in the coaching manual

Lacking that Half Yard of Pace – Kind way to describe a player who should be a bit quicker than he is for his position, and will probably be moved on in the summer

Lacklustre, A Bit – A manager's favourite to describe a team that had shown no spark or spirit

Lambast – Only a referee can be lambasted, and only a manager can do the lambasting. No one else in modern society lambasts

Last Chance Saloon – One of the poorer clichés. A cliché must relate to something familiar to its audience.

No football fan has ever failed to find a saloon for a drink

Last-Ditch Defending – Like the Royalist troops against Cromwell's men at the Battle of Worcester in 1651 – from where the expression comes – this is when the team under siege hang on grimly to protect the goal

Last-Gasp Goal – When fans have drawn their final breath of the encounter, and a goal goes in. Man United fans famously had the joy of breathing two last-gaspers in the 1999 Champions League final against Bayern Munich

Last Man – Lone defender against an overwhelming attack with no option but to hack down his opponent and take a red card for the cause

Latch On – When a player receives a pass

Lay-off – The shortest of passes, about as far as a waiter serving a plate

73

Leave the Foot In – Euphemism for an horrendous tackle. See Also **Ankle-snapper, Studs-Up**

Left Nothing on the Pitch – What players claim to have done in a losing cause so no one can fault them for effort

Legend – Often abbreviated to 'Ledge', and prefixed by 'Club' - or the nationality of the player - this tends to refer to any player who has been in the game for more than twenty years. See Also **Giant of the Game**

Let the Ball Do the Work - When everyone in the team is taking up good positions and passing the ball as they are meant to

Letter of the Law – Strict interpretation of the rules as laid down by the **Man in the Middle**

Libero – Fancy term for a tall, ambling defensive player who can pass the ball accurately over a range of ten yards and be trusted to sweep up all the loose ends

Lighthouse Up Top - Big centre-forward. See Also **Old-Fashioned Nine, Target Man**

Line-o – A very marginally quicker way of saying Linesman

Liquid Football – Even runnier than 'fluid football'

Little Bit Lacking in Certain Areas – *Euph.* i) Manager's subliminal appeal to the club to **Open the Chequebook**

and buy half a dozen players to replace the shit ones he's having to make do with ii) Manager's polite post-match lament that half his team played crap

Loan Player – Stop-gap player taken by skint clubs who can't afford to pay the full whack for him … Or an unwanted player a club can't sell … Or a talented youngster farmed out to a lower league club so he can get bashed around a bit and come back mature and hardened

Loggerheads, At – Usually of clubs haggling over a transfer fee

Lollipop – Old-school for a step-over

Long Ball Game – None of that poncy stuff playing it on the carpet. Just get it up there and have a crack

Long-Suffering Fans - Picture a sea of faces in Everton's Gwladys Street Stand

Loose Pass – Nice way of saying 'Shit ball' that misses its target by yards

Low Centre of Gravity – Fancy way of describing a tiny player, usually stocky

Luck, Riding His – When a **Scrapper** or **Guvnor** is haring around the centre park hacking down any player anywhere near the ball

Lull – Euphemism for an extremely dull period of a game

Lump – A farmer's kick out of defence

Lung-Bursting Run – Any sprint up field longer than fifty yards, often fruitless, leading to the explosion of respiratory organs

Luxury Player – A class act who can't lower himself or be bothered to tackle or track back

Lynchpin – Everyone loves a lynchpin. That often unglamorous player who somehow makes the team whole, his qualities becoming obvious when he's not playing

M

Made it Hard for Us – Translation: 'We were always going to beat this crappy little side, but they had a decent spell for five minutes either side of the break.'

Magic of the Cup – Once a truism that spoke to every football fan in the country, now sounds more like a desperate marketing logo for the FA Cup, whose glory has been diminished by the rise of the Premier League and Champions League

Magic Sponge – Playful expression for physio's on-pitch treatment of a player who springs back into action, his knock not as life-threatening as first feared. They did once use sponges

Magic Wand – What the angry manager of a struggling club doesn't have to wave around to sort out the dire problems he faces

Magnificent, The Fans were – Never 'Marvellous' or 'Splendid', certainly never 'Not Bad' or 'Just About Alright' and definitely not 'Absolutely Shit', a club's fans (usually midweek travelling ones) are magnificent when they keep up an incessant wall of noise and abuse about everything and everyone connected to the opposition

Makeshift Defence – When there's a midfielder in the back four and a towering centre-back at full-back

Manager's Faith – What all players are morally bound to repay

Managerial Merry-go-Round – Key attraction in football's off-field funfair when the fans get to watch the spectacle of clubs hiring and firing managers because they're bored or frustrated by the current one. See Also **Musical Chairs**

Man in the Middle – You'd hope the ref got around a bit more than that. He's only really in the middle right at the beginning

Man Manager – A manager with more communication skills than giving his players the **Hair Dryer Treatment** and throwing teacups around

Man-of-the Match Award – Moment of panic when the TV co-commentator must pick out the one player who has done something notable in the game, beyond the terms of his contract or expectations. Usually, the bloke who scored the deciding goal

Man On! – Warning hollered to alert a teammate that an opposing player is bearing down and about to clatter him from behind. Do players still shout this, or has the game become too fast?

Man-to-Man – i) A marking system ii) Chat between manager and player to settle their differences

Marathon not a Sprint – The oft-heard reminder by a manager after yet another defeat that there are still twenty-odd games to go, and please don't sack me quite yet

Marauding – Only full-backs are allowed to maraud

March On – Like a conquering army laying waste to all resistance it encounters, when a team has won three or four games on the trot

Marching Orders, Receiving – Like a red-carded player has ever actually marched from the pitch arms swinging as if on the parade ground

Mare, Having a – Of a player, usually a goalkeeper or centre-back, who has made two or more massive blunders

Massive Club – The status of every club a new player has just joined, usually one that won the FA Cup in 1924 but nothing since

Masterclass – When a team that can pass the ball properly hammer one who can't

Mauling – When a team has torn another to shreds leaving only a carcass of dignity

Mazy Run – When a player goes around at least two players. **Dribbling** at its best

Meat and Drink – Of a straightforward save by a keeper or goal by a striker. Pah! It's what he does. See Also **Bread and Butter**

Medical – What the incoming player must undergo before signing on, and everyone is hoping the scan doesn't reveal degenerative arthritis or an underlying heart condition

Megged – Slang of the slang word **Nutmeg** when a player puts the ball through a player's legs and causes him deep embarrassment

Men Against Boys – When a team of big hairy macho types batters one of craven, pre-pubescent lads

Mental Strength, Good – Modern parlance for when a team has shown a bit of **Character** and not folded when they've gone behind

Mercurial – Of a hugely inconsistent player with a lot of talent who does something really impressive every tenth game

Mexican Wave – The sign of a dull game or a Noddy club, a phenomenon hated by true football fans who refuse to get out of their seats to join in the 'fun'

Mickey Mouse Cup – Contemptuous term for any knockout competition other than the FA Cup

Midfield General – Authority figure, usually scary, calling the shots in the midst of battle

Midfield Maestro – Extravagantly gifted player who conducts the play and brings harmony to a team

Mind the House – The job of the **Defensive Mid** while the Attacking Mid goes shopping

Mind Games – PsyOps in the enemy camps when rival managers mess with each other's heads before a big match, often with a little dig but usually by over-praising a team or the man himself, hoping complacency will set in, thereby ensuring victory will be all the more impressive

Minnow – This species of footballing fish is only to be found in the FA Cup, usually a tinsy, little backwater club no one has ever heard of in a town no one visits unless they have to

Mixer, In the – Vivid expression for a ball into the box that is sure to cause a frantic whirl of activity and panic

Moment of Magic – That little bit of sorcery that rescues an otherwise turgid encounter

Monitoring – You have to be a transfer target or a player recovering from injury to get monitored

Monopoly Money – What clubs spend on players these days. See Also **Silly Money**

Mug Off – Make an opposing player look stupid

Mulling – When managers and chief financial officers stroke their chins, look into the middle distance and contemplate the purchase of a player

Musical Chairs - When a clutch of managers all move round one to the next **Hot Seat**

Muted Celebration – When a player scores against the club he had served since he was a kid and is pretending he's breaking up inside and not at all delighted to have scored against the bastards who transferred him after all those loyal years

Mutual Consent – When a player accepts that he's shit and agrees to leave the club without a penny

N

Nailed On – Of a penalty so clear that the truth of it has already been hammered in, and if the ref doesn't give it, then he's a blind man who's lost his marbles. See Also **Out-and-Out, Stonewall**

Name on the Cup – When the trophy engraver can get on top of his To Do list because one team is walking the final. See Also **One Hand on the Trophy**

Natural Goal Scorer – Not one of those new-fangled AI ones

Near Post/Back Post – Reference to one of the uprights, usually when the keeper has been beaten at one of them and should have done better. See **Stick**

Needless – Of a foul on a player

The New - ... Messi, Beckham, Ronaldo, Gerrard... the burden on any young player who shows a bag of talent. Rarely fulfilled. The lower leagues are littered with 'New

Rooneys' just plying a trade

Never Know When They're Beaten – Even when they've been battered five-nil, less intelligent teams walk off thinking they've won

New Manager Bounce – When a side with a new man in the **Hot Seat** wins their first couple of games before reverting to its losing streak. See Also **Honeymoon Period**

Never Stopped Believing – Reflection of a player, flush with excitement, caught in the tunnel after scoring a late winner, like he's a pop singer introducing his next number

Neymaring – Rolling around as though repeatedly stabbed after a light challenge. Named for Neymar, the brilliant Brazilian playmaker and, to some, a preening prima donna

Nick a Goal – Why buy one when you can just nick it when no one's looking?

Nightmares - … about that for years to come. Of a player missing an easy chance

No Easy Games at this Level – Manager's unconvincing claim after seeing his team beaten by the bottom club

No-Look Pass – What the cool players do, not even bothering to look up or check it reached its intended target. Often performed by a player with **Eyes in the Back of His Head**

No-Man's Land – Of a player, usually a forward, wandering around aimlessly, or a terrible pass into an area where there isn't a player for 30 yards

No-Nonsense – Of an **Old-Fashioned** challenge that leaves the opposing player lying on the ground writhing in agony

Nodded Off – When a dozy defender or goalkeeper drifts off and a goal is scored

Normal Service Resumed - Train timetable metaphor describing the end of a period of disruption when the

favoured team regains a lead they had somehow contrived to lose

Normal Time – There's still about ten minutes to play

Nosebleed, Get a – Of an unskilled defender daring to venture forth over the halfway line and get creative, the idea being he is boldly scaling heights of achievement beyond his ability

Not at the Races Today – Odd, well-used expression to describe a team that has underperformed. Well, where were you?

Not Getting Ahead of Ourselves – When a team has won a couple of games at the start of the season

Not Happy at All – Massive understatement by a manager of a referee's decision or a terrible performance by his team. Rough translation: I'm effing furious and when I'm off camera I'm going to start kicking and smashing things up

Not that Sort of Player – When a usually angelic player dives or commits a terrible foul

Not the Quickest – Commentator's euphemism for a player who lacks the speed to be playing at that level

Numbers Going Forward – When lots of players head towards the opposition goal

89

Numbers (Making them Up) – Of a player in the side because there is no one better available

Nut!, On the – Imperative to deliver a cross on to the player's head

Nutmeg – Guaranteed to raise a cheer from the stands, when a player makes an opponent look foolish by slipping the ball between the opponent's legs and collects it on the other side of him. See Also **Megged**

O

Obstruction – When a player forgets to get out of the way and there's a good break on

… Of this World – 'The Man Us and Man Citys, your Arsenals and Chelseas …'

Off the Back of – A long-winded way of saying 'after'

Off-the-Ball Incident – Sneaky little back-street assault in the shadows when the perp hopes no one important is watching

Off the Bench – From the days when all substitutes sat on a wooden bench and not in a massive, padded armchair

Off the Park, Played – Nice old expression when a team has been swept aside so that their presence on the pitch has been barely noticeable

Offside! – Choral cry from one end of a ground when an oppo player streaks towards goal

Offside Trap – Do they still lay traps?

Old-Fashioned – Usually of a Cup tie, a hideous tackle, or the big lump of a centre-forward

Old-Fashioned Nine – Massive centre forward with limited skills but good at heading. See Also **Target Man, Lighthouse Up Top**

Old Head on Young Shoulders – A player of precocious wisdom

Old Stomping Ground – A player's former club. An old expression referring to the area of a field where cattle like to gather and stomp about

Olympic Goal – Scored directly from a corner after an Argentinian player did exactly that against Uruguay at the 1924 Olympics

On a Sixpence – The tiny area of space on which a player pivots rapidly

On Toast – When a player, usually a fast winger, has the better of the man marking him

One or Two Players Short, Probably – Lugubrious lament of the manager who keeps losing games by tight margins

One-Club Man – Player who spends their entire professional career at one club and will therefore eventually become its manager, or the match-day host if they have struggled with drink after **Hanging up their Boots**. See Also **Stalwart, Absolute**

One Game at a Time, We're Taking it - How else? Two at a time?

One Hand on the Trophy – As full time in the final approaches and the side in the lead is in total control. See Also **Name on the Cup**

One-on-One – When the striker must score, but often doesn't because he **Fluffs his Lines**

One-Touch Football – Slick play, the ball passed around with none of that schoolboy trapping or fannying about looking for options

One-Two, Little – Neat passing interchange between two players sanding very close to each other, usually on the edge of the **Box**. See Also **Give-and-Go**

One-Way Traffic – When the lights are stuck on green one way and red the other

Onion Bag – Poetic old-fashioned word for the goal

Open the Chequebook – When the chairman or club is obliged to spend money on new players. More likely an electronic international bank transfer with a SWIFT code today. Many young fans will never have seen a chequebook. See Also **Splash the Cash**

Open Goal – A space 7.32m by 2.44m that some players inexplicably contrive to miss

Orc – Northern fan, according to a southern one

Out-and-Out – Usually of a penalty. See **Stonewall, Nailed On**

Out of the Blocks – A team is considered quick out of them when they score an early goal or create a host of chances

Outhouse – Massive player. See Also **Big Old Unit, Hammer Thrower, Colossus, Physical Freak**

Out on their Feet – A team utterly shredded after being given the run-around by a superior side

Overcook – Of a pass with too much heat

Over the Moon – What football managers used to be after a victory

P

Packhorse – Unglamorous player burdened with the heavy lifting. See Also **Grafter, Piano Carrier, Dirty Work, Beaver, Workhorse**

Panenka – A penalty kick chipped over the tumbling keeper rather than placed or blasted. Named for Czechoslovak Antonín Panenka, who dared to score like that against West Germany in the final of the 1976 Euros

Parachute Payment – Financial cushion given to clubs relegated from the Premier League to soften their landing in the Championship … to the deep irritation of the clubs already down there

Parking the Bus – A phrase that took a matter of months, weeks even, to graduate to full-blown cliché. Like the best clichés, it is self-explanatory. Coined by manager José Mourinho, annoyed that Tottenham put all their players in defence to thwart his Chelsea side

Part and Parcel of the Game – A catch-all phrase employed to describe any regular feature of the game whether we like it or not

Parting Ways – Diplomatic announcement by a club that they have sacked their hopeless manager

Peach, Absolute – Usually of a great pass, but also a goal. Like a **Beauty**, a peach must be absolute

Pear-shaped, It's All Gone – When a side's fortunes take a dramatic turn for the worse: commonly a sending-off, followed by two quick goals and a bit of a scuffle in the Away end. See Also **Wheels Coming Off**

Pearler – A beautiful shot, often said of a 'curler', probably owing to poetic word association in the commentator's mind. A more powerful, direct shot is usually a **Belter**

Pecking Order – Like hens in the farmyard, cocky young footballers must respect the seniors in the hierarchy and wait their turn at feeding time

Peg Back – Score an equaliser. Origin uncertain, possibly naval, when a flag or colours were lowered to a 'peg' below, indicating a reduction in status in the fleet

Pen – i) Penalty kick, usually **Nailed-On**, cast in iron or solid as a **Stonewall** ii) *Verb*. A player *pens* a new contract

Pepper – When a team enfilades the goal with shots, often in a bid for a **Last-Gasp** winner

Phantom Goal – The reason why VAR was adopted. When a ball crosses the line and is not given by the blind bastard in black. See Also **Ghost Goal**

Philosophical in Defeat – When a manager keeps his temper in check in the post-match press conference

Phoenix Club – A club built on the ashes of an old one, e.g. AFC Wimbledon

Physical Freak – A massive player, usually a gym monster in defence or a player who runs all afternoon like he's on crack. See Also **Hammer Thrower, Big Old Unit, Colossus, Powerhouse**

Piano Carrier – The player who does all the hard graft and heavy lifting so that the more skilful fancy-pants players can put on a performance. See Also **Packhorse, Dirty Work, Grafter, Workhorse**

Pickpocket – When a player uses stealth to nick the ball and **Mug Off** his unsuspecting victim

Piledriver – A shot so powerful it is thought to resemble the heavy plant equipment used for pounding holes in the earth for the construction of bridges and piers

Ping – To fire a sharp direct pass, no messing about

Pitch Invasion – When fans of a backwater club that has experienced no success for over a half century, contravene the law, spill over the hoardings and do star jumps all over the pitch before being chased away by men in Hi-Viz bibs

Planning a Raid – When officials in the club's command bunker move little toy footballers around with croupier sticks before making a bid for a player

Plate, On a – What a **Meat & Drink** chance is served on

Play Acting – Rolling around on the grass like a dog with an itchy back

101

Play to the Whistle – To keep up the tempo until the shrill, sustained blast of the ref's little plastic mouth organ

Playmaker – The skilful player in the team

Play-off Final – A trip to Wembley after nine months of agonising tension, ending in unfettered joy for one club, and abject misery for the other

Play Out from the Back – Is there any other way?

Plot (Losing it) – When brains turn to salad, the **Wheels Come Off** and it all goes **Pear-Shaped**

Ploughing a Lonely Furrow – When a striker is abandoned by his teammates and occupies himself with heavy farmwork to pass the time in the **Acres** of space up front

Poach – i) To pounce and snatch a goal from under the nose of the gamekeeper-goalkeeper ii) To acquire a player from another club in a slightly underhand manner

Poacher – A cross between a **Pickpocket** and **Goal hanger**, milling around minding his own business, possibly whistling, then pouncing to grab a goal from short range

Pocket, In his – The place a defender tucks a striker to keep him under control and stop him from causing mischief around the goal

Poisoned Chalice – Commentator's go-to Shakespearean term to describe a manager's ominous task at the desperate club he has just joined

Powerhouse – Big lad at the back

Poznań, Do the – Weird celebration by which fans turn their back on the pitch. Huh? First seen at Polish club Lech Poznań, since adopted at Manchester City

Pragmatic – Euphemism for a dull, defensive approach to the game

Prawn Sandwich Brigade – A military-style unit of bourgeois fans who eschew traditional pies for seafood products in focaccia. Phrase coined by fiery ex Man United skipper and TV pundit Roy Keane

Pre-season Friendly – Randomly organised matches against local non-league sides and obscure overseas outfits

Pressing – When the defenders get **Nose Bleeds** and start pushing up the pitch towards the dizzy heights of the opposition half

Prima Donna – Highly talented, oversensitive player who wears gloves in Spring and falls over in light south-westerlies

Professional Foul – Poorly chosen phrase, giving the stamp of officialdom to the offence of an intentional foul. See Also **Cynical**

Profligate – Only a misfiring striker can be profligate, wasting chances with abandon

Proper Pies – The consolation of Away fans travelling to a remote club in the North

Prowl – Only a technical area can be prowled and only by a manager rubbing his chin

Psychological Blow – Usually of a goal scored just before the break

Pub Team – Disparaging term for a side playing like a bunch of pot-bellied, hungover misfits from the Rising Sun. See Also **Sunday League, Farmers' League**

Pulsating – A game positively throbbing with action and incident, so please don't go channel-surfing during the ads

Purple Patch – Classical reference to the imperial purple to describe ten minutes of half-decent football

Pushovers, No – Manager's diplomatic speak for the visit of a shitty team who will put up a fight for the first 20 minutes then get battered

Put in a Shift – When a team or player rolls up the sleeves and puts in a workmanlike shift before clocking off for a pint

Puts Himself About – Of a player who would be wearing an electronic ankle bracelet if he wasn't kept under control by a football club. Slightly unhinged, often diminutive midfielder who hares around chopping down opposition all afternoon. Usually can't pass or shoot straight. See **Add Some Steel, Guvnor, Hardman, Enforcer**

Pyramid – Questionably helpful word for any formation that isn't 4-4-2 with a lone striker representing the pointy bit at the apex of the human polygon

Q

Quality – As an adjective to describe a side, or a player

Queuing Up – Orderly line of players waiting patiently to score the easy goal

Quick Feet – Of a footballer with more agility on the ball than others

R

Rabona – Not to be attempted at home, and definitely not on the way back from the pub, this is an expert's skill of contorting the body by wrapping the kicking leg around the back of the stationary one. Serves no obvious purpose other than showing off

Raft of Substitutions – Two or more replacement players make a raft

Raking Pass – Long pass, usually cross-field. 'Raking' because the player has to pull his leg right back and sweep into contact with ball, as he might have seen his gardener doing for real at his executive mansion

Rate – Football doesn't admire a player. It rates them. No need to add 'highly'

Really Good Account of Ourselves – Spoken by a bouncy manager after a surprisingly good performance by his team

Real Striker's Goal – As opposed to those facsimile ones you get these days

Rearguard – When the first advances have been repelled and losses suffered but the lads regroup and rally

Recycling the Ball – Slightly irritating new term for passing the ball around, inspired by the second bin in our drives

Red Mist – When a player is consumed by a frothing rage, does something daft or dangerous, and finds himself in the shower five minutes later reflecting on his moment of madness

Reducer – Stupid word for a crunching tackle early in a game designed to intimidate a player and establish a sense of dominant purpose

Ref – Often short, busy little man with a whistle in his mouth, two watches, a notebook and a deck of cards who gives up his weekend afternoons and weekday evenings in order to be abused by thousands of strangers

Refused to Rule Out – Of a previously tight-lipped manager edging towards a confession he fancies a young midfielder at Peterborough

Reinforcements – Players brought in during the transfer window to bolster flagging troops

Resilience – A quality that has been creeping into post-match speak in recent times, slowly edging out old classics like 'some character' or 'good spirit'

Results Business, We're in the – Manager's curt dismissal of any suggestion that his team are dull to watch after his team have ground out a stalemate or a joyless 1-0 win

Right Way, Playing Football the – Passing it along the ground, no cynical or dirty stuff

Riot, Running – When a team starts torching the oppo and looting the scoreline, gleefully running off with an armful of goals

Rise, Meteoric – You can rise up the ranks or the standings at a steady rate, but it's far more exciting to rocket there like a meteor. The meteoric rise is often followed by disintegration and a plummeting to earth

Robbed – When the better is team is downed by a late goal and the cruel caprice of fate

Rock at the Back – Heroic defender against whom the opposition has broken itself trying to pass. See Also **Stalwart, Absolute**

Rocking Horse Shit, Rare as – Of a goal by a defender

Roll, On a – When a club gathers an irresistible momentum. Three victories on the trot, or five unbeaten, is the minimum requirement to qualify for this descriptor

Rollercoaster - Of an erratic performance or run of form when the team reaches great heights and then plunges the depths, week after week

Rolls-Royce – A tall, experienced midfielder who ambles around the centre circle making short passes sideways

Ronglish – The colourful and rich lexicon of former manager and pundit Ron Atkinson, sacked in the end for a being a little too colourful

Rotating the Squad – A luxury enjoyed by the richer clubs, allowing the star players to have a nice massage and facial and get their nails done

Round-robin – Twee name for the group stages of a competition. Phrase comes from old French, *Rond Ruban*. Don't worry about it. It's not interesting

Rounding the Keeper – Easier said than done

Route One – How the British used to play football until the fancy continentals invaded with their slick passing and movement. Direct football: lump it up field, knock the defender out of the way, smash it in the net. See Also **Kick & Rush**

Row Zed – The distant seating area where long-range efforts or clearances by **No-Nonsense** centre-backs come to rest

Roy of the Rovers Stuff – Unbelievable football drama when a team comes from 200-Nil down to win, or a 12-year-old comes on to score a five-minute hat-trick in the Cup Final. Refers to the long-running comic strip. Roy had to retire in 1993 after losing his left foot in a helicopter crash

Rub Down, A Good – The pleasure awaiting aching footballers after the match. It's that, or an ice bath

Rue – When a player is cursing, gobbing and pounding the turf after **Fluffing his Lines** and squandering a **Meat & Drink** chance served to him **On a Plate**

Rusty – A nice way of saying a player has returned from injury too soon, or a team is hopelessly under-prepared after the summer break

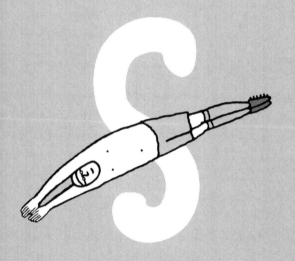

S

Sack of Spuds – The way footballers used to hit the deck after a heavy challenge. No one used to fake it back in the days of real men, proper boots and **Proper Pies**

Sack Race – Weird phrase… Like managers burst out of the blocks desperate to be the first to lose their job

Safe Pair of Hands – A solid, unspectacular goalkeeper good under a high ball

Safety – What fans of clubs menaced by relegation long for after nine months of agony

Scapegoat – The player singled out as the cause of failure after one costly error when in fact the whole team was crap

Schoolboy – Unfair slight on the schoolboy community for a comical mistake. Do schoolboys make more errors than adults? Used as an adjective, dropping the 'Error'

Scissor Kick – Similar to a **Bicycle Kick** only the airborne player is on his side and not upside down

Scorcher – A shot with some heat on it

Scoring Goals for Fun – When a striker is having the time of his life laughing the ball into the net over and over again

Scorpion Kick – Ridiculous acrobatic kick when the player lunges forward and strikes the falling ball forward with his heels; one for the beach rather than attempting in a real match. Aside from Olivier Giroud's brilliant half-Scorpion (one heel) for Arsenal in 2017, the 'Scorpion' is just cheap thrills and showing off

Scrapper – Often short and ginger, the scrapper will pinball himself around the centre of the park, hacking and clattering and getting **In the Face** of the opposition

Scrappy, A Bit – All-too-common term to describe the first half of a match

Screamer – A long-range goal struck with such power it makes a Horror-film noise

Script, You Couldn't Write a – When events are so outlandish a Hollywood screenwriter wouldn't dare to present it as a credible plot

Scruff of the Neck – When a player has had enough of the fannying-around he will seize the game and give it a good shake

Scruffy – Of a goal that has come off a shin or knee

Sea of … – Name your colour. When a stadium of one end is chock full of fans parading the club colours

Seal Dribble – When the circus comes to town. A sight rare as a **Scorpion Kick** and about as useful. The show-off player flicks the ball up and runs around bouncing the ball on his head. Why?

Second Season Syndrome – When the promotion bounce has gone, the better teams have worked out you're a team of shit imposters way out of your depth and you need to go back to the Championship forthwith

Seen That?, How's He Not – Manager or commentator's lament that the ref's blindness has missed a **Stonewall** penalty or blatant foul

Seen Them Given – When the co-commentator, who has been around the block a few times, tells viewers that he has witnessed many a penalty awarded for an innocuous challenge

Set Piece – When the game pauses for about five minutes, the players shove and pull each other's shirts in the defensive wall, and there's an argument about who's taking the free kick, and finally the ball sails up to **Row Zed** and the game can restart

Sew – Another metaphor borrowed from embroidery to describe a sequence of passes that **Stitch** together to make an attractive move. See also **Weave, Thread**

Shackled – When a defending player puts an attacking one in a form of restraining device

Shambolic at the Back – Commentator's go-to expression to describe a bit of confusion in the **Box**. See Also **Comedy of Errors**

Shank – Term borrowed from golf to describe a horrible mis-kick at goal, or a keeper's clearance

Sharing the Spoils – When the teams meet after a drawn game to distribute the golden goblets and heraldic shields

Shepherding – When a defender steers an attacker away from the goal area without making physical contact, like a sheepdog rounding up a stray sheep into a pen

Shergar, Done a – Of a player who has gone missing in the game. After the famous racehorse stolen by the IRA

Shielding – When a defender walks the ball into touch fending off the bloke pressing into his backside and kicking his ankles, or a player is down at the opposition's corner flag trying to run down the clock

Shimmy – Usually a little one. Wafting the boot around to wrong-foot the defender

Ship - Concede goals like a boat taking on or 'shipping' water

Shocker – One-worder, requiring no further explanation, to describe a player or team's wretched performance

Shoot! – Crowd plea when the player is about 20 yards out, the ball lined up nicely and nothing to block its path into the roof of the net

Shootout – After 120 minutes of action and half a dozen matches to graft into the final, when the colossal effort is settled by a semi-lottery

Showdown – i) A contest between two big teams, or a crucial encounter ii) Of talks between the manager or club with its want-away star player

Shoulder, Looking over Their – What clubs do when they are just above the relegation zone

Shut up Shop – When a side has gone in front and decided to hang up the Closed sign, their goal no longer open for business

Shutout – An extremely **Clean Sheet** when the opposition haven't had so much as a dribble on goal

Shuttle Runs – The fruitless sprints back and forth made by a full-back waiting for someone to pass to him the ball

Sick as a Parrot – What managers in sheep-lined suede coats used to be after an ill-deserved defeat but are too embarrassed to say today for fear of mockery. An expression long overdue a revival. Everyone loves a sick parrot

Sickening – Only a clash of heads can be sickening

Side's Going to Turn Up, Don't Know Which – Unpredictable team, brilliant one week, dreadful the next

Sighter – When a player first adjusts his range with a speculative effort, like an artillery gunner bracketing a target

Silence the Critics – When the misfiring striker finally finds the back of the net, puts his finger to his lips to call for hush among the fans and an eerie silence descends over the stadium… and 10,000 men give him the w***er gesture

Silly Money – A ridiculous sum of money to squander on an average or unproven player. See Also **Monopoly Money**

Silly Season – The summer break when clubs spend madly, players return from the beach to play strange teams in remote outposts in pre-season warm-ups

Silverware – Generic word for trophies in football including those made from gold like the World Cup, and the cheaper alloyed ones of lesser competitions

Simulation – Posh word for diving

Sit up Nicely – What a well-brought-up ball will do so that the player can have a lovely clean strike on goal

Sit the Keeper Down – When a penalty-taker feints, the keeper falls on the floor like a clown and the ball is stroked into the net

Sitter – The easiest of chances when it's just sitting there asking to be scored

Sixes and Sevens at the Back – Chaos and confusion in defence. Phrase comes from a medieval dice game

Six-pointer – Crucial league game towards the end of the season usually between two close rivals fighting to avoid the drop, or at the top, vying for the title or promotion

Skied It – When a shot is mistakenly struck towards the heavens instead of the goal

Skin – When a very fast player is said to takes a sharp knife to a slow one and leave him for dead

Skip – Skipper, Captain

Skip By – Fanciful description of a player who has rounded another without a care in the world

Slalom – When a tricky player weaves his way through the static obstacles in defence

Slams Shut – A **Transfer Window** can never be quietly closed and latched, but it never shatters in spite of the great force applied

Slapped with a Ban/Fine – A player or manager is never given or issued one; he must be slapped with it about the chops. An entire club can get a slap

Slapping a Price – Likewise, players are never given or marked with a transfer price. As with bans and fines, it is essential the cost to the buyer is slapped like a wet haddock

Slide Rule Pass – A pass of perfect precision that not even a hand-held mechanical calculator can better

Slide Tackle – When the player comes in on his bum

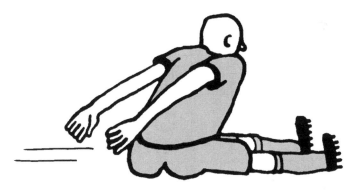

Slippers – Modern football boots, not like the proper ones with wooden soles and nails from the good old days

Sloppy – Usually in reference to a pass or casual defending

Slot Home – Neat finish, usually with the inside of the foot

Smash & Grab – Like a robber at the glass counter of a jewellery store, a team seizes its one opportunity and runs off with the ill-deserved spoils

Sneak Something Here, Might – When a team on the back foot for most of the game steps up their performance and starts probing for chances

Sniper, Shot by a – Disparaging term when a player goes down like a **Sack of Spuds** under a featherweight challenge

Socks, Running Them Off – When players have made such an effort over the 90 minutes that their foot clothing comes away

Soft – Of a referee's decision to award a penalty or a foul that didn't merit sanction

Soft Goal – There is no 'hard goal' opposite, but the soft one comes because there was no one in the **Wide Awake Club**

Something Nobody Wants to See in Football – When fans roll back the years to the 1980s and start knocking lumps out of each other in the stands and throwing seats, or storm the pitch with menacing intent

Sorry Display – An almost sympathetic summary of a team's performance, usually at a club going from bad to worse

Spark, Need of a – When a flat display or dire game needs some ignition to set in on fire

Speculative Effort – A weak, wayward attempt on goal when there's not much going on, and why not?

Speed Merchant – A player who purveys quick pace for a living. See Also **Blistering Pace, Flying Machine, Genuine Pace, Jet-heeled,**

Splash the Cash – When a club pays over the Recommended Retail Price for a player, or goes on a spending spree like a drunk with a fresh credit card at Christmas

Spray the Ball Around – What the club pays its **Midfield Maestro** to do

Square Ball – Lateral pass, effectively keeping the play on pause, testing the patience of fans if it's done one too many times in succession

Squeaky Bum Time – Tense, final moments of game when fans make a funny noise squirming around on their small plastic seats

Spine – The key players running through the centre of the team formation, the vertebrae being the keeper down at the coccyx, the **Old-Fashioned Nine** up by the head, with the **Midfield Maestro** and the **Defensive Mid Guvnor** or **Towering** centre-back stiffening the middle

Spineless – Pathetic team performance when some players have failed to **Turn Up** and others just didn't **Fancy** it

Stalemate – Chess term to describe a match in which neither side was able to break out and score a goal

Stall (Setting it Out) – Like a costermonger laying out his veg at dawn, when a team makes its purposeful intentions for the day early in the game

Stalwart, Absolute – i) Player who has been at a club since he first got pubes ii) … at the back. When a defender, usually a centre-back, has seen off all trespassers. See Also **One-Club Man, Rock at the Back**

Statement of Intent – A major signing signalling a club's vaulting ambition

Statement, Make a – When an out-of-favour player gets the chance to prove he's worth it

Stay on your Feet – Advice to a player being buffeted by angry defenders

Steaming In – Usually a big lad tearing in at the back stick for a header, or a midfielder making a hideous challenge

Step-over – A sort of non-skill when the player airs his foot over the ball in the hope of fooling the man marking him. See Also **Lollipop**

Stick – Post, front or back. A player never hits his shot against a Stick, but he can arrive at one or deliver a cross there

Stinger – A hard shot that would probably smart if the keeper wasn't wearing nice thick gloves

Stitch Together – When a team puts together a string of passes into a coherent pattern. One of several textile metaphors in the football lexicon. See Also **Weave, Sew, Thread**

Stonewall – A penalty claim so strong you could build a wall to retain livestock with it. See Also **Nailed-on, Out-and-Out**

Stoppage Time –See **Added Time, Injury Time**

Straight Red – Penalty for an offence so terrible, usually an atrocious foul, that a caution won't even touch the sides

Strings (Pulling Them) – Like a puppet-master, when the **Midfield Maestro** works his teammates to put on a virtuoso performance

Strip – A team's playing **Kit**

Strong Words – What the players can expect in the dressing room at half-time

Student of the Game – Manager who has read books about football to improve his knowledge

Studs-Up – Even the word hurts. When a player hurtles into the ankles of an opposition player baring the sole of his boot

Stunner, Absolute – A stunning goal must be 100 per cent of itself, otherwise it's just a **Scorcher**. See Also **Screamer, Belter, Banger/Beauty**

Style, Turning On the – When a team goes all fancy and starts stringing together moves with multiple passes and cute little flicks

Sublime – Only a pass, generally a long one, can be sublime

Sublime to the Ridiculous – Great goal at one end, then almost at once a howler at the other

Suck the Ball into the Net – Often said of the Kop at Liverpool, this is when the will of the fans for a goal has been so urgent, they are credited with inhaling it into the **Onion Bag**

Sucker Punch – A boxing term for when the team in control is caught off-guard and concedes a goal against the run of play

Sudden Death – When the next kick in a form of penalty shootout will decide the fate of a long, hard-fought contest

Suicidal Back Pass – Over-the-top description of an idiotic pass to the keeper that will probably lead to a goal, and the death of the player's credibility

Suitors – Transfer targets, like beautiful princesses, always attract swooning love-struck Romeos below their balcony

Sunday League Football – Insulting term to describe a low-quality performance by professionals who should know better. See Also **Farmers League, Pub Team**

Supersub – Player with a habit of coming off the bench and scoring crucial goals, encouraging the belief he has special powers

Surplus to Requirements – A player moved on or tossed onto the transfer list because he's no good, or there are five better players in his position

Surprise Package – A team that happily exceeds all expectations in a competition, like an unexpected gift in the post

Survival – The objective of most teams in a division at the start of a season. See Also **Safety**

Sweeper-Keeper – Once the traditional role of a designated outfield player, in modern football the goalkeeper has come to take on the sweeping role of this second last line of defence, coming out of his box to tidy up and add an extra passing option

Swashbuckling – Only a midfielder can swashbuckle like a pirate; of a flamboyant player who will play with bravado and daring or not at all

Sweep Home – A particular type of goal, generally a flourishing or tidy finish at the end of a fluid move from deep

Switch It! – Urgent exhortation to move the play from one side of the pitch to the other

T

Table Does Not Lie – Even when it says Leicester are top and Brighton fourth

Tabs – What a club keeps on a player of interest to them. Bonus fact: Shepherds used to keep 'tabs' on their crooks to keep count of their flock

Tactical Nous – When something goes right on the pitch and the manager is credited with being a mastermind of great cunning

Tails Up – When a team is surging forward like dogs to their bowls at feeding time

Take Apart – Like mechanics methodically stripping down an engine, a team dismantles the opposition with professional efficiency

Take a Touch – When a goal-bound ball takes a slight deflection off a player

Take it one Game at a Time – Has a team ever taken them two or three at a time?

Take on Fluids – Footballers don't drink these days; they take on fluids

Take One for the Team – The questionably honourable act of hacking down a player through on goal and being shown the red card

Take Out – Merciless hitman job on an innocent man minding his own business

Tapping Up – When a club makes an unauthorised approach to a contracted player, the deal agreed in a Little Chef on the motorway. Former Notts Forest manager Brian Clough loved it: 'We have tapped up more players than the Severn-Trent Water Board.'

Target Man – Big, strapping lump of a centre forward with the close skills of the Honey Monster, good in the air, only in the team for his physical presence and aerial ability. See Also **Old Fashioned Nine, Lighthouse Up Top**

Teacups – The go-to projectile of the angry manager at half-time

Team to Beat – Favourite in a competition, or the one enjoying a hot streak of form

Technical Area – Small boxed area around the dugout for caging managers to stop them careering up and down the touchline and bellowing abuse at the Line-O

Technician – A player who goes about his footwork like a precision engineer

Teckers – Street word for accomplished technical skills

Tempo, Up the – When a team has had enough of the slow movement and, presto, there is some pace and urgency in their rhythm

Terraces, On the – Generic phrase describing the fans in attendance, still in use in England in spite of stadiums going all-seater in the early 90s. A postage stamp of a 'safe standing area' to satisfy a club's noisy mob has been permitted since 2022/23

Testimonial– Historical tradition of rewarding a retiring player for his long service at the club with the gate receipts from a friendly match, usually against the club's bitter rivals. Less common today because top players earn more in a week than most once did in an entire career

Textbook – When footballers apply what they first studied in the classroom

That's Football – Meaningless expression to describe any kind of setback. Basically, 'Tough shit, no one said life is fair.'

There for the Taking – When a team becomes vulnerable to a hungry predator

They All Count – A scruffy little goal or fluke that cannot be downgraded for being crap or lucky

Third Man Running – Decoy runner to paralyse a defender with indecision

Thrashed - A team is said to have received a rawhide whipping when it loses by five goals or more, and the players are left red-faced and smarting

Thread Needles – Yet another embroidery image in football to describe a player lacing **Through-balls**

Thrills & Spills – When a football match turns into a kid's fourth birthday party

Through-ball – Pass threaded as if with a needle between two defenders

Thunder Bastard – A very powerful strike on goal. Or 'Thunderc**t' at the less refined clubs

Thunderbolt – Root word of **Thunder Bastard**

Tide, Turning It – When the ebbing is over, and the team starts to flow

Tight-lipped – When the whole world knows a club are trying to buy a player, but managers and clubs seal their mouths

Tiki-taka – Annoying little expression from Spain describing a smug style of play with short passes and silky little players slipping into 'channels.' See Also **One Touch**

Toe-to-Toe – When teams go at each other like boxers

Toe Punt – What you're expressly told not to do as a kid. The rules are more relaxed right in front of a goal when a 'toe poke' is fine

Too Good to Go Down – Of a club with a massive squad of underperforming players hovering over the **Drop Zone**

Too much Respect, Showed Them – A diplomatic way of saying a team lacked fight or belief

Toothless – No bite in a performance by a team likely also to be missing its spine, its gut and any number of clues

Top Bins – Life borrowing from art here, with this new buzz phrase meaning the top corners of the goal, taken from a game played on Sky's Soccer AM in which participants must volley into real bins

Top Drawer – From where a player draws his most precious items. Weirdly, there's no Junk Drawer in football

Top Flight – Where the high-flying teams like to cruise and look down on the rest

Total Football – Technically, a fluid style in which any outfield player can take over the role of any other player, as patented by the Dutch in the 1970s, but it has come to mean any passage of play in which more than a dozen of passes is strung together

Touch, Good First – When a player can receive a pass without it bouncing off his shin

Tough Place to Come, Always a - Diplomatic talk for a crappy club everyone can beat in their sleep but must respect because they won the League Cup in 1972

Towering Header – When a ball is headed goalwards by a large man suspended in mid-air

Tracksuit Manager – An old-school manager who loves his cones and bibs and likes to get down and dirty with his players on the training ground rather than leave the playing part of football to a suite of coaches

Trade, Plying his – Like a plumber or electrician with an honest job, a player is said to be plying his trade in his specialist field position or is doing so now at a new club

Trailing Leg – What a wicked player catches when he **Leaves His Foot In**

Training Ground, One From the – Whenever a team scores from a set-piece, it is assumed that the players have worked tirelessly on the tactic of one of them delivering the ball into the box and another heading it in

Transfer Kitty – A tiny little **War Chest** for buying players

Transfer Limbo – A purgatory between Heaven and Hell where unsigned, out-of-contract players live

Transfer Window – Short for 'window of opportunity' - otherwise the mid-season period in which clubs can buy players it describes is just something clubs can look through

Transitioning – Pompous new phrase with no obvious definition, when a team has to readjust from attack to defence or *vice versa*

Trap – i) Basic skill of securing pass with the sole of the boot ii) A cunning scheme by defenders to snare a player in an offside position

Travelling Army of Fans – The battalions of belligerent men in nylon uniform marching into the Away Stand ahead of a battle in which they will be only noisy observers. See Also **Twelfth Man**

Treble – i) Three major trophies in a single season ii) George Best's half-time refreshment

Trigger (Pulling it) – When the player has the goal in the crosshairs and it's time to take a shot

Trying to Walk it In – When a player wants to look cool, but takes too long and is denied an easy goal

Tuck Away – Neat finish, generally nice and snug into a corner

Tunnel – Where the players come and go beneath the main stand, holding hands with small children on the way out for a big match; dishing out verbal abuse and occasionally throwing fists on their return

Turn up (Failure to Do So) – When a team played so limply they might as well have not bothered coming

Turning Point – Moment, according to losing manager, which explains the 5-0 rout e.g. the first goal, sending off, the pen not given

Twelfth Man – A nod to the fans who gave such encouragement they were as effective as an extra player and at one point actually **Sucked the Ball into the Net** with a collective intake of breath

Two-footed Tackle – As ugly as it gets on a football pitch. No one accidentally goes into a challenge with both boots

Two-Horse Race – When Manchester City and Arsenal turn into the final straight

Typical Forward's Challenge – Commentator's forgiving take on a lumbering forward's hideous challenge. See Also **Clumsy More Than Anything**

U

Ugly head, Rearing its – When there's a tear-up in the stands and the commentator worries we're heading back to the 1970s

Ultras – Continental hooligans who carry knives, set off flares in stadiums and can't see the game because they have unfurled a pitch-size banner over their heads

Unacceptable – Of a transgression that no one wants to see **Creeping Into the Game**

Unbelievable Belief – When the commitment just shown on the pitch defies articulation

Underachievers – A poor club that thinks it's better than it is

Underdog – The runt in the dogfight all set for a good mauling by the big scary one

Under the Cosh – When a team trembles under the blows of a short nineteenth century truncheon

Unveil – When a club summons the press and pulls off a sheet to reveal, hey presto, another disappointing journeyman midfielder

Up for Grabs – When the fate of the game is up in the air

Upset – The emotional state of the fans after watching their side lose to a **Pub Team** in the Cup

Utility player – Bits-and-pieces player not good enough to hold down a regular position but useful for plugging gaps when the injuries mount up

V

Vanishing Spray – Can of magic shaving foam refs carry in a holster to spray on the grass at a free kick to stop defending players encroaching. Pepper spray is the next step

Vein of Form - Usually a rich one for a striker **Scoring Goals for Fun**

V.A.R. – Short for Video Assistant Referee, the man who keeps interrupting and slowing down the game

Virtual Spectator – … at the other end. Goalkeeper whose team are doing so well, it's getting a bit boring and lonely

Vote of Confidence, The Dreaded – No manager wants to hear the club's board making the effort to issue a statement to declare their faith in him. Foreign Office-speak for: You've got two more games, muppet, or you're out on your ear

Vuvuzela – Form of torture to make people turn off their televisions and radios. Deeply annoying, plastic horns blown by supporters at the 2010 World Cup in South Africa, never to be heard again

W

Waffle Stomp – Studs-up tackle that leaves its mark on the opponent's calf

WAG – A blow-up plastic doll that footballers carry around to international tournaments, often with big lips and massive sunglasses

Wake-up Call – Manager's euphemism after his team have suffered a 5-0 hammering

Wall – A set-piece feature for players to push, pull and strangle each other

Waltz – When a twinkle-toed player sashays through the defence

W**ker – Fans' word for the ref

Want-away – Of a player who has not hidden his desperation for a transfer from his awful club

War of Words – Long-distance combat conducted through the Press between clubs or their managers. See Also **At Loggerheads**

War Chest – The gold reserves of a big club about to **Splash the Cash** on major new signings. Lesser clubs must make do with a poxy **Transfer Kitty**

Warhorse, Old – Grizzled and scarred **Stalwart** pumped with cortisone who has given the game his all

Wayward – Commentator's forgiving description of a shot landing in **Row Zed**

Weave – Describing the elaborate movement of a player in and around the penalty area, or a player **Threading Needle** passes

Weight – The gravitational force applied to a football by a boot for a pass …

… Welly, Give it Some – When a tremendous amount of gravitational force has been applied to the ball

Wet Wednesday Night in Wigan – Generic phrase for any southern team who quails at the prospect of a midweek fixture in a derelict mill town up North

Wheels Coming Off – What happens to a team after the splutter of the engine and before the crash

Whimper, Without a – When a team is perfectly happy to be beaten

Wicked Deflection – A deflection with bad conscience and no mercy for is victims

Wide Awake Club – You're in it or you're not, dozing or fully alert to what's going on around you

Width of The Park – The area players are encouraged to use so that the ball can do the work

Win is a Win, A – Manager's defiant statement of the obvious after an ugly struggle against a lesser team

Wing Wizard – Mythical figure from the good old days who slicked his hair with Brylcreem and smoked fags at half-time. They're all **Marauding** full-backs who **Take on Fluids** these days

Wipe the Floor With – When a poor team is used like a floor cloth, their faces rubbed in the dirt

Withdrawn Role – A forward asked to drop deep, often never to be seen again in the course of the match

Wonder Goal – An absolute **Scorcher** from back in the day that Dads bore their sons about

Wonderkid – Brilliant young player carrying an intolerable burden of expectation

Woodwork – What shots cannon off because it's more poetic than saying Polypropylene

Work Rate – Measurement of a player or team's effort haring around to get the ball

Workhorse – The player who does all the hard work and **Puts in a Shift** for the fancy players. See Also **Grafter, Dirty Work, Pack Horse**

Workmanlike Win – Dull display for the three points and everyone goes home a bit deflated

Worldy – Slightly annoying fresh cliché that has shot from nowhere describing a goal considered to be world-class

Worth the Entrance Fee Alone – When a great goal or a **Moment of Magic** is priced by the commentator at about fifty quid

X, Y, Z

X-rated – Of a tackle so brutal only people over the age of 18 should be allowed to witness it

Youngsters Watching, For Any – Learn that, kid, and you too could be driving a baby Bentley

Your Rooneys and Beckhams of this World – Collective description for great players. Also of big clubs … Your Arsenals and Man Citys

Yo-Yo club – A club that bounces up and down between the divisions, stuck in a kind of Purgatory of mediocrity, too strong for the Championship but never good enough to settle in the Premier League

Zombie Football – Excellent, vivid description for a clueless team wandering about the pitch with its arms held out in front of them

Acknowledgements

This being the third in the series of Badger sports glossaries, I have already run out of superlatives of acclaim to thank illustrator Mudd Bexley. When I heard that she had been shortlisted for the World Illustration Awards, the only surprise was that she had achieved that great feat at the start of her career. Most people have to wait decades, and then get no accolades at all. I can no longer say she is star of the future because she is clearly one of the present. She is brilliantly inventive, very funny and a true professional.

The design duo of Rebecca Brown and Andrew Brown have once again gone about their work with stolid, unflappable efficiency, imaginative flair, patience and wisdom. Going from strength to strength, they have recently changed the name of their business from Design for Writers to Principal Publishing to reflect the expansion in their operations. Check them out at www.principal.pub.

About the Author

Niall Edworthy is one of the UK's most prolific authors and successful ghostwriters. A former reporter for broadsheet newspapers and the international wire agencies AFP and Reuters, one of his first beats was covering English football in the early 1990s. He also covered the 1998 World Cup and the European Championships in 1996 and 2000.

Niall began writing books in 1997. His first book was *England: The Official FA History*, his third *The Second Most Important Job in the Country*, the story of England's managers and the trials they endured. He is also the author of the best-selling football classic *S**t Ground No Fans* under the pen name Jack Bremner.

He is the author or ghost of almost 50 titles, most for the big publishing houses, many of them for well-known names (actors, soldiers, musicians, sportsmen & television personalities), others for 'ordinary' people with extraordinary stories. He has written in a wide range of genres, mainly Biography, History and Natural History but also Humour, Sport and recently, in Fiction. His first novel, Otto Eckhart's Ordeal, was shortlisted for the Wilbur Smith Best Published Novel Award 2021. He will soon be publishing his second novel. He lives in West Sussex, UK.

If you enjoyed *Badger's Football Slang and Banter*, you might also enjoy *Badger's Cricket Compendium* and *Badger's Golf Compendium*

NIALLEDWORTHY.COM

Printed in Great Britain
by Amazon